source

Also available from Church House Publishing:

Life Attitudes
Life Balance

Robert Warren //
Kate Bruce

LIFEsource

a 5-session course //
on prayer //
for Lent //

✠ CHURCH HOUSE PUBLISHING

Church House Publishing
Church House
Great Smith Street
London SW1P 3NZ

Tel: 020 7898 1451
Fax: 020 7898 1449

ISBN-13 978-0-7151-4094-9
ISBN-10 0 7151 4094 9

Published 2006 by
Church House Publishing

The opinions expressed in this book are
those of the individual authors and do
not necessarily reflect the official policy
of the General Synod or The
Archbishops' Council of the Church of
England.
Cover design by S2 design and advertising
Printed by Creative Print and Design Group
Ebbw Vale, Wales

Contents

Acknowledgements

The authors and publisher gratefully acknowledge permission to reproduce copyright material in this book. Every effort has been made to trace and contact copyright holders. If there are any inadvertent omissions we apologize to those concerned and will ensure that a suitable acknowledgement is made in all future editions.

Transcript on page 67 reproduced by kind permission of the Archbishop of Canterbury, © Rowan Williams 2005.

Extracts from the New Revised Standard version of the Bible, Anglicized Edition, (NRSV): copyright © 1989, 1995 by the Division of Christian Education of the National Council of the Churches of Christ in the United States of America, and used by permission. All rights reserved.

Scripture quotations taken from the Holy Bible, New International Version. Copyright © 1973, 1978, 1984 by International Bible Society. Used by permission.

Extracts from The Archbishops' Council of the Church of England, Common Worship: Services and Prayers for the Church of England (2000) and Common Worship: Daily Prayer (2005) are copyright © The Archbishops' Council of the Church of England and used by permission.

Extracts from Praying Through Life (second edition), by Stephen Cottrell, copyright © 2003. Used by permission of Church House Publishing.

Extracts from How to Pray, by John Pritchard, copyright © 2002. Used by permission of SPCK.

>> Introduction

>>Who is this course for?

Life Source explores the practice of prayer. Many Christians do not need convincing of the value and gift of prayer but most of us at some point or other may need help in our prayer lives. Those setting out on the journey of faith will want to find ways of developing their new-found relationship with God. Those who have been on the journey for some while know how easy it is to get stuck, and want to find refreshment for their prayer life. For some, even getting as far as praying is beyond them; as a cartoon caption put it: 'I am a great believer in prayer. I pray almost every day of the week. Almost on Monday, almost on Tuesday, almost . . . !'

>>The aim of the course

The course aims to encourage group members to discover a new-found joy and delight in prayer, to find that it really is our 'Life source'. Each session of *Life Source* uses a Bible study, along with a range of interactive activities to introduce and explore different ways of praying drawn from our rich Christian heritage. Group members are also encouraged to try out new prayer patterns and practices between sessions. As Elizabeth Obbard puts it: 'You learn to pray by praying.'[1]

>>Why pray?

The truth is that prayer is an incredible gift. The God who 'flung stars into space'[2] invites us to meet with him.

What is amazing is that we do not avail ourselves more fully of this heavenly friendship – through prayer. Jesus himself modelled this: for him, prayer was truly his 'life source'. For him, prayer was about:

---

1. *To Live is to Pray*, Elizabeth Obbard (see *Bibliography*).
2. From 'The Servant King' by Graham Kendrick.

> enjoying a relationship with God, seen as Father;
> engaging in a listening process in which we come to 'know and be known' by God;
> experiencing a totally secure loving relationship with the One who is the source of life and love;
> receiving help (grace), wisdom (insight) and guidance (direction) from beyond ourselves and our resources;
> daring, because of the reality of the love experienced, to make ourselves totally available for God to direct our lives.

For Christ, and his followers, prayer is not an end in itself but the means to a greater end, namely, living in the reality of the presence of God.

Maybe prayer is the hidden wiring of the human life
that connects us to the world wide web of the Spirit.

John Pritchard, How to Pray, *p. xiv*

>>What does the course consist of?

There are **five sessions** for group study, each designed to last 90 minutes. Each session covers one major aspect of a balanced prayer life. Relationship with God is approached by looking at how human relationships work and then building on that. Each session also introduces one or two prayer patterns – different styles of praying.

> **Session 1: Source of Life: prayer as relationship**
  An overview of prayer seen as a relationship with God within a framework of *seeing–knowing–going*. The 'Getting in touch' and 'Lord's Prayer' prayer patterns are introduced.

> **Session 2: Source of Joy: prayer as enjoying God**
  Prayer involves stepping outside ourselves to pay attention to God, through thanksgiving, praise and adoration. A 'Stepping into worship' prayer pattern is introduced.

> **Session 3: Source of Light: prayer as listening**
  A real knowing of God takes us beyond the familiar realms of worship and intercession, to listening to God through Scripture. The prayer pattern introduced here is based on the *lectio divina*, a way of listening to the Scriptures.

> **Session 4: Source of Wholeness: prayer as honesty**
  How we can listen to God in the whole of life, and face the
  truth about ourselves and our broken world. This session's
  prayer pattern is based on the examen, a 'review' prayer.

> **Session 5: Source of Love: prayer as care**
  This session explores how, through prayer, we can give
  expression to God's love for us and all creation. The prayer
  pattern uses a biblical blessing as a model for praying for
  others.

>>How each session works

Material for the course is in two sections for each of the five sessions –
Beforehand and *The Session*. The *Beforehand* section is aimed at leaders
and provides all they will need to prepare the session.

Beforehand contains:

> **Aim** of the session – to help focus preparation and subsequent
  evaluation of the session.

> **What you will need.** A checklist of practical materials. See
  pages 10–12 for a more comprehensive list of resources.

> **Background.** This gives an introduction to
  the aspect of prayer being explored in this session;
  the Bible passage being studied;
  the prayer pattern used in the session.

Some groups might like to read this material during the session or in
advance. Alternatively, it can be summarized by the leader at the
appropriate *input* sections in the session.

The Session is structured under the following headings:

 Welcome

 Drawing near

 Time to share

 Encounter: studying the Bible together

 Do something

 Go deep: prayer patterns

 Get going: prayer practices

 Extras

There is enough material for a 90-minute session. However, do remember that some of the material is optional and it is better to pick and choose and do a few sections well than rush through everything and leave the group exhausted!

If you have a shorter amount of time, then we suggest that you focus on the following sections:

Welcome
Drawing near: use the course prayer
Encounter
Go deep
Get going

Each session follows this same structure. The sections of the session work in the following way.

>>Welcome (10 minutes)

The leader welcomes the group and puts people at their ease. If your group is one that is meeting for the first time, it is important – at the first session – to make sure everyone knows the others in the group. Session one contains suggestions for doing this.

For the rest of the course, after the initial welcome, there are two things groups can do. First is to look back and share insights from seeking to do the prayer practices from the previous session. The second is to look forward to the theme of this session by exploring a question in response to a quotation about prayer in the text.

Either of these can be omitted: it all needs to be kept moving, lasting a recommended ten minutes for the whole section.

>>Drawing near (10 minutes)

This is the **opening prayer time**. Clearly, with prayer as the subject of the course, it is important not to miss this out. This time should also act as a 'stilling' time, allowing group members to recover from the busyness of the day and the rush of getting to the meeting! A particular prayer pattern is suggested to kick off each session. A course prayer (the same for each session) is provided for those who prefer that option, or groups may want to develop their own pattern of prayer here. Background music is appropriate for some of the prayer patterns. Suggestions are given in the Resources section (pages 10–12).

>>Time to share (10 minutes)

This is a conversation time to reflect together, either as a whole group or in pairs, about some aspect of human relationships. Questions are suggested to help group members explore how they relate to others, applying these insights to the question of how they can know God better.

>>Encounter (25 minutes)

This section has three elements:

> **Input:** a short talk from the leader (or other person) based on his or her reading of the *Background*. Alternatively, group members may prefer to read the *Background* themselves.

> **Read:** the Bible passage. Get someone else to do this – but ask the person before the meeting.

> **Talk about it:** questions are supplied to help the group explore the passage. You can introduce your own questions here. Split into groups of three if the whole group is large.

>>Do something (20-30 minutes)

Many people grasp things best by seeing or doing something rather than just talking about it. Here is their opportunity. *A number of options are provided – choose one.* This section needs careful planning. Again, consider asking someone to handle just this aspect of the session. Feel free to shorten and adapt here.

>>Go deep: prayer patterns (10 minutes)

This section encourages groups to 'go deeper' in their prayer lives. A different prayer pattern is provided each week. These exercises are drawn from our rich Christian heritage and involve people's bodies, senses and creativity.

For some this will be a completely new and perhaps uncomfortable way of praying. Some will question why it is sometimes good to use structure in prayer and to develop a pattern. Essentially there are two types of prayer – the *extempore* (or 'free') and the *set form*. Extempore prayer is a great way to express to God what we think and feel; but we can get into a rut if we limit our prayers to that form. Set prayers can take us beyond the familiar and be a real help when we don't feel like praying (for example, in times of illness or when we hit a dry patch), but they can lapse into dull routine.

The prayer patterns provided in these sessions use an interplay of 'form' and 'freedom', seeking to draw on the riches of both approaches. They help us to focus prayer while allowing us space to pray silently, or the freedom to extemporize around particular themes. Using a structure with words that people can say together includes everyone – those who feel confident with extemporizing and those who feel less so. Handled well, the prayer patterns can provide focus and freedom, creating a secure yet stretching experience of prayer.

Leading the prayer pattern

Full instructions are given in *Beforehand* and *The Session* sections to enable the leader to guide the group through the exercise.

>>Get going: prayer practices (5 minutes)

This course will be of most benefit if group members are encouraged to get going: to try out prayer patterns and new prayer practices themselves between sessions. So, in this section, a range of different ways of engaging with prayer are suggested. You should use this time to discuss which ones you will agree to have a go at before the next session.

Note: Leaders should treat the suggested timings for *Go deep* and *Get going* as flexible and feel free to divide the 15 minutes allocated to these two sections differently, depending on what suits the group.

>>Extras

Supplementary material for each session is provided at the back of the book. Group members may want to read this for themselves. You could also photocopy the relevant pages from the book, or print out copies from the web site.

>>Practical matters

Group size

An ideal size for a group studying the course would be between 8 and 12 people. Larger groups may well find it helps to divide into small groups for some of the discussion aspects.

To get the most from the course, we suggest that each group member has a copy of the book.

Who can lead the course?

Most people, with a little preparation and thought, could lead this course. The leader's main task is not to teach or lecture the group, but to enable discussion and exploration by group members by leading them through the material provided.

Leading a group can be a big task for one person, so look to share the tasks around with others. These include leading the prayer times, leading the *Encounter* section, or the *Do something* element, as well as providing hospitality and refreshments.

Where should we meet?

Wherever you meet, make sure the room is comfortable, warm and easy for everyone to get to. If splitting into two groups, do so in separate rooms if space allows, as two groups in the same room can be distracting. However, three or more groups can often work in one room, especially if each group sits close enough to hear each other without raising their voices. Be aware of the hard of hearing who can find background noise makes hearing more difficult.

You may like to provide refreshments before or after the sessions. Be aware that extra time needs to be added to the 90-minute recommended time for the session.

To help lead the group we offer some tips below. The booklet *Leading an Emmaus Group* (see *Bibliography*) is a real help with this task.

>>Tips for leaders

Be prepared

Make sure you are familiar with the material. Read through both the *Beforehand* section and *The Session* itself. Decide which parts you will use, given the amount of time available and the nature of your group. If you want to use any of the multimedia or more interactive suggestions, you will need to source the materials: a list is given at the start of the *Beforehand* section. You will also need to decide whether to work in smaller groups for some of the activities, and if you need to ask others to help with some of the sections.

Using the background material

The background material (see *Background reading* below) can be used to supplement the *Beforehand* notes. Both are to help the leader lead the session. It is best not to read out from any source in the session, but to put background ideas and information into your own words. The aim of the sessions is to help people explore the subject and practice of prayer. The goal is not to tell people what to think or do, but help them to discover those things by working together on the material provided.

The Input part of the *Encounter* section needs preparation beforehand. Keep it brief, making a few points clearly. The more you practise what you are going to say, the less you will need to simply read out notes.

Delegate

Don't do everything yourself: share out tasks with others. Not only does this help the leader, it gives others the chance to develop their gifts as leaders. Invite others to read the Bible passage, do the refreshments or welcome people. If you plan to work in groups, invite someone to lead each group. In view of the importance of the prayer element in this course, consider asking someone to lead the times of prayer (*Getting in touch,* and *Go deep: prayer patterns*).

Give people plenty of warning. Don't land them with difficult jobs at the last minute. Be available to give support and advice if needed. Give them the chance to look at the material beforehand.

Be organized

> Get to the venue in good time so that you are not doing last-minute preparations as people are arriving.
> Set the room up carefully so there is room for everyone and they can all see each other, the leader, flipchart, video, etc.

> Make sure you have all the pens, paper, craft materials, music, and objects beforehand. Note the checklist at the start of each *Beforehand* section.

Be imaginative

People learn in different ways: some take in information by reading and quiet reflection, others through discussion; others respond best to visual stimuli (so value a visual focus for worship); others respond best through music, craft, or doing things. The course provides you with a range of resources to work in these varied ways. We encourage you not to do what is easiest for you but what is likely to be most productive for the group. Be inventive and draw on your own and the group's creativity.

>>Resources

Background reading

There are many helpful books on prayer, but this course draws on three in particular. Each of them puts the emphasis on giving practical help in prayer. They are:

Stephen Cottrell, *Praying Through Life*, second edition, Church House Publishing, 2003.

John Pritchard, *How to Pray*, SPCK, 2002.

Robert Warren, *An Affair of the Heart,* second edition, Highland, 1999.

The bibliography at the back of the book gives detailed references to related background material, in these books and elsewhere. Having any one of these books is a good basis for a leader's preparation, and can be recommended to participants as a follow-on.

Music

We have suggested that you use music sometimes to prepare for prayer both at the *Drawing near* and *Go deep* sections. The following recommendations may be useful:

> **Taizé** several CDs are available, including *Wait for the Lord* (Gia, 1995);

> *Instrumental Praise* Series of CDs (Brentwood, 1999);

> *Smooth Classics* (Classic FM, 2002);

> *Moon, Sun and All Things* (Hyperion, 2005), especially track 16, 'Dulce Jesús mío';

> *Global Journey* (North Star Music, 1996).

Some specific pieces of music for the *Stepping into Worship* prayer patterns are:

Stepping into worship

You could use *Chillout Worship 2004* (Authentic Music), as background music for each of the three sections in this prayer practice:

> *Give thanks* – 'I shall not want' (Andrew Green/Wendy Green, 2003);

> *Give praise* – 'From all that dwells', (Andrew Green/Wendy Green, 2004);

> *Give yourself* – 'Breathe' (Marie Barnett, 1995).

Or you could use any other worship CD that picks up the three key themes of this prayer practice (thanks, praise, giving yourself to God).

Objects

There is a list at the beginning of each of the *Beforehand* sections of what you will require for the session, but feel free to be creative!

Images

If you want to use images of Christ as a visual focus, try:

> *The Christ We Share* pack (CMS/USPG), which contains over 30 images of Christ.

> *The Faith We See*, Janet Hodgson (Methodist Publishing House, 2006) – a good guide to using images and contains a CD with 20 images of Christ.

> **Icon postcards** – many cathedrals, churches or religious bookshops sell postcard images.

> **www.google.co.uk** Click on images then enter *Christ, icons of Christ, Christ healing, Christ teaching, Christ praying, contemporary Christ,* for a vast range of images you can download and print out.

>> 1 Source of Life: prayer as relationship/Beforehand

>>Aim

This session looks at prayer as a relationship with God, drawing on insights from our relationships with other people to help us in our praying. As in any human relationship, an initial encounter leads to a 'getting to know you' phase and on to an experience of life enriched by meeting that person.

The session also introduces two prayer patterns. See page 00 for a fuller explanation.

What you will need (make your own selection)

> Candles;

> Music (see pages 10–11 for suggestions);

> For the *Do something* activities:

Option 1: copy of Rublev's icon. This can be obtained on a postcard (available in some Christian bookshops) or via an Internet search engine (*images – 'Rublev's Icon'*);

Option 2: slips of paper each with a line from the Collect for Purity;

Option 3: lining paper, scissors, glue, recent newspapers and magazines.

>>Background

Leaders: see pages 8–10 for ideas about how to handle individual elements of the sessions.

Session background: prayer as relationship

The Scriptures are full of stories of people meeting with God, from Adam and Eve in the garden to John on the isle of Patmos in the book of Revelation. Each is unique: yet there is a pattern, for it is the pattern of all relationships, as much with others as with God. That pattern can be described in the following terms.

First is a *seeing* of the other: The handshake, kiss or hug, and eye contact are ways we pay attention to and notice others.

Second is the *knowing* stage where an exchange takes place. It may be stories of what we have been doing, or a deeper sharing of thoughts, feelings, hopes and fears. It may be superficial ('Nice day isn't it?'), or a profound exchange ('I couldn't say this to anybody else, but . . .').

Prayer is about exploring a relationship with God,
not about perfecting an esoteric technique.

John Pritchard, How to Pray, *p. 15*

Third is the process of *going* in the light of that meeting. We are affected in some, often seemingly small, ways. We go with a lighter step or heavier heart: cheered, puzzled or better informed. With God we always go *with*, not *from*, him.

The course takes us through each of these three stages, exploring how they work out in human relationships and in our relationship with God in prayer.

Bible passage background:
Moses at the burning bush (Exodus 3.1-12)

Notice the *seeing–knowing–going* dynamic is at work in this story.

The *seeing* is certainly dramatic – a burning bush. He will have seen bushes burning before in the desert, but never one *not* consumed by the fire. Moses realizes God is here, that this is holy ground. He gives God his full attention.

The *knowing* process begins with introductions. Moses is called by name, and God declares his name/nature ('The God of your father . . .'). The Lord knew that Moses was himself burning with righteous indignation about the slavery his people suffered. He had given fatal expression to that consuming fire through killing the Egyptian. Now God reveals a righteousness no less strong than that of Moses, but full of tender compassion for his people: 'I have observed the misery of my people . . .

heard their cry . . . know their sufferings and I have come down to deliver them.' This compassionate righteousness will take deep root in Moses' soul as the story progresses. The profound knowing has begun.

The *going* phase comes as a real shock: '*I* have come down to deliver them . . . so come, I will send *you* to Pharaoh.' Moses is being co-opted into God's plans for his people. Vocation to share in God's loving purposes is always the fruit of a true encounter with God.

Prayer pattern background: The Lord's Prayer

In this session, the Lord's Prayer is used as a framework for our own prayer.

There is a fourfold shape here that can help in praying this familiar prayer.

> **The address:** Christ teaches his disciples to call God 'Father' to show what sort of relationship we are to have with him. We are to pray 'our' Father, not 'my' Father, since, even in private prayer, we come before God as part of his family. Honouring God's name involves reflecting his character in all of life.

If we were to change the Lord's Prayer from the third person to the first, it would not just diminish the prayer, it would destroy it.
A prayer of mutual generosity would become one of narrow selfishness.
Stephen Cottrell, Praying Through Life, *p. 18*

> **The you-prayers:** The focus is on God's purposes (kingdom/will). Here, conversion to Christ is expressed in prayer, as we dedicate ourselves to what God wants, seeking first the kingdom of God.

> **The us-prayers:** We bring our needs to God: *material* ('give us'), *relational* ('forgive us') and *spiritual* ('deliver us'). They are the needs of those who, having dedicated their lives to overcoming evil with good, know their need of God.

> **The affirmations:** Though added later by the Church, they underline the truth of which we need reminding – that Jesus is with us 'to the very end of the age'.

>> 1 Source of Life: prayer as relationship/The Session

>>Welcome (10 minutes)

This session looks at prayer as a relationship with God, drawing insights from our relationships with other people to help us in our praying. It also introduces two new prayer patterns to help us pray: 'Getting in Touch' and one based on the Lord's Prayer.

Prayer is the most natural thing in the world. It can also be the hardest. Because it is relationship it is about letting go and allowing someone else to be at the centre of your life. In so many ways the human spirit will recoil from this kind of loving. We like to be at the centre ourselves.

Stephen Cottrell, Praying Through Life, *p. 11*

What are the most 'natural' or 'hardest' aspects of prayer for you?

At the start of this course you could share your thoughts about prayer by completing one or more of the following sentences.

I think prayer is . . .

I think the purpose of prayer is . . .

The hardest thing I find about praying is . . .

The most important influence/help in my prayer life has been . . .

>>Drawing near (10 minutes)

Create a still atmosphere. You might like to light a candle, play some music and use the following *Getting in touch* prayer pattern and/or use the course prayer.

Slowing down is a vital part of the spiritual journey . . . that's what we're terribly short of in our culture – space to let quiet things breathe.

John Pritchard, How to Pray, *pp. 5 and 6*

Busyness is a great obstacle to prayer; yet our busyness is best cured by stopping and taking time to pray. This prayer pattern helps us slow down, set the busyness of the day aside, and turn our attention to God.

The *Getting in touch* prayer pattern works best if:

> we put books, etc. aside so that our hands are free;
> the leader says all words in ordinary print (omit the headings, which are in **bold**);
> the leader takes unhurried time, leaving space for silences.

Words in *italics* may be used as prompts by the leader as appropriate.

Getting in touch

Sit upright, relax and breathe slowly. Put both feet on the floor and rest your hands on your thighs. Start with your palms facing down.

Palms down: letting go

Let your hands express your giving to God . . .

> *The tasks, relationships, activities and struggles of this day.*
> *Any sense of guilt or failure about your prayer life.*

We are not abandoning these things but putting them into the hands of the God who assures us that 'underneath are the everlasting arms'. *(Deuteronomy 33.27, NIV)*

Now, we turn our palms up in an attitude of receiving.

Palms up: taking hold

Let your hands express openness to what God wants to give . . .

> *the gift of his presence;*
> *insights and guidance to help us in our prayer.*

St Augustine said: 'God gives where he finds empty hands.'

Be still:

Let's stay in God's presence and enjoy his welcome. (Repeat, slowly, two or three times) 'Be still and know that I am God.'

Course prayer

Thanks be to you,
Lord Jesus Christ,
for all the benefits you have won for us,
and all the pain and insults you have borne for us.
O most merciful Redeemer, Friend and Brother,
may we see you more clearly,
know you more dearly,
and follow you more nearly,
now and for evermore. Amen.

adapted from Richard of Chichester

>>Time to share [10 minutes]

Think of someone whose friendship you value: a friend, family member, partner or spouse. What is it you value about that relationship? What do you get from this friendship and what do you put in to make it work? You could do this in pairs, or as a group.

What do you value about your relationship with God?

Human beings are made for relationship with God. When we pray we discover the truth about ourselves: that we are children of God. Within this relationship we can flourish and become fully ourselves as God intended us to be.

Stephen Cottrell, Praying Through Life, *p. 11*

>>Encounter [25 minutes]
a. Input: prayer as relationship [5 minutes]

Use the background material (pages 13–14) to introduce the idea of the three stages of any relationship as *seeing, knowing,* and *going.*

b. Read (5 minutes)
Moses at the burning bush (Exodus 3.1-12, NRSV)

[1] Moses was keeping the flock of his father-in-law Jethro, the priest of Midian; he led his flock beyond the wilderness, and came to Horeb, the mountain of God. [2] There the angel of the Lord appeared to him in a flame of fire out of a bush; he looked, and the bush was blazing, yet it was not consumed. [3] Then Moses said, 'I must turn aside and look at this great sight, and see why the bush is not burned up.' [4] When the Lord saw that he had turned aside to see, God called to him out of the bush, 'Moses, Moses!' And he said, 'Here I am.' [5] Then he said, 'Come no closer! Remove the sandals from your feet, for the place on which you are standing is holy ground.' [6] He said further, 'I am the God of your father, the God of Abraham, the God of Isaac, and the God of Jacob.' And Moses hid his face, for he was afraid to look at God.

[7] Then the Lord said, 'I have observed the misery of my people who are in Egypt; I have heard their cry on account of their taskmasters. Indeed, I know their sufferings, [8] and I have come down to deliver them from the Egyptians, and to bring them up out of that land to a good and broad land, a land flowing with milk and honey [. . .] [9] The cry of the Israelites has now come to me; I have also seen how the Egyptians oppress them. [10] So come, I will send you to Pharaoh to bring my people, the Israelites, out of Egypt.' [11] But Moses said to God, 'Who am I that I should go to Pharaoh, and bring the Israelites out of Egypt?' [12] He said, 'I will be with you; and this shall be the sign for you that it is I who sent you: when you have brought the people out of Egypt, you shall worship God on this mountain.'

c. Talk about it (15 minutes)

See background notes on pages 14–15 of *Background*. Consider some of or all the following questions:

> **Seeing:** Moses sees the burning bush and through this meets with God. *What helps you to be aware of God? Do you have a particular experience to share of how you have been drawn to God?*

> **Knowing:** God knows Moses' flaws and failings (see Exodus 2.11-12). God is the one 'to whom all hearts are open, all desires known' (from the Collect for Purity* – see page 24 below for the text). *Given all that he knows about him, why do you think God still chose Moses? Given all that he knows about us, why has God chosen us?*

> **Going:** God uses the concern Moses already has and puts it to positive use. *Looking back, can you see times when a similar pattern has been true in your experience or in the lives of others you know of? What should we do when, like Moses, we feel really angry about some injustice?*

>>Do something (20–30 minutes)

Try **one** of the following activities:

> **Seeing:** Put a picture of Rublev's icon in a central position. Explain that it is a representation of Genesis 18, when three angels visit Abraham. Explain how the icon also works as an image of the Trinity, with the fourth space, in the foreground, representing God's invitation to us, to step into relationship with him. Play some music and allow people to study the picture and reflect on this invitation.

> **Knowing:** Write each line of the Collect for Purity* on a separate slip of paper and hand the slips out to different group members. Play some quiet background music. Read the whole collect through to the group, pausing at the end of each line. Then have the collect read again using different voices, with a pause at the end of each line. Finally, read the whole collect again to the group. Ask people, in pairs, to share any words and phrases that struck them.

(*A collect is a type of prayer used in some traditions to gather people together in prayer at the start of a service.)

> **Going:** Make a prayer collage: lay out a roll of lining paper in the centre of the room and provide PVA glue and a selection of recent newspapers and magazines. Ask people to select images, headlines and articles about which they feel a strong sense of concern. When the collage is complete, ask people to

stand back, look at it as a whole and share any thoughts about how the collage inspires them to pray.

>>Go deep: prayer patterns (10 minutes)
A pattern for praying the Lord's Prayer

Rabbis gave their disciples a prayer that summarized all their teaching. Jesus is doing that in this prayer. In it (see page 15 for further background) he teaches his disciples to:

> call God 'Father';

> seek his kingdom;

> look to him for daily bread, forgiveness and strength to overcome evil;

> and trust his presence with them always.

This prayer can:

> be repeated word for word;

> be used as a framework for our praying;

> provide headings for a more extended time of prayer.

Introducing the prayer pattern

Either invite people to read the above introduction to the Lord's Prayer, or summarize it for the group.

Explain that the following prayer pattern uses the Lord's Prayer as a framework for our praying, with space for our own prayer.

Words in ordinary type are said by the leader.

Words in **bold** are said out loud by all.

Words in *italics* are prompts for personal prayer, and may be read out by the leader as appropriate.

Allow silence for personal prayer and reflection between each section.

Praying the Lord's Prayer

Leader: Let us pray to our Father in heaven.

> > *we worship God who made us, knows us and loves us;*

> > *we honour and delight in God as Father, redeemer, guide . . .*

Leader: Our Father in heaven:
All: hallowed be your name.

Leader: let us pray for the coming of God's kingdom.

> > *we give thanks for God's loving purposes for all creation;*

> > *we offer our lives to be part of God's purposes in his world.*

Leader: your kingdom come,
All: your will be done, on earth as in heaven.

Leader: Let us pray for our needs as disciples of Christ.

> > *let us be specific in bringing our practical needs to God;*

> > *where we've been wrong, own it and receive God's forgiveness;*

> > *if we have been wronged, admit it and release it to God.*

Leader: Give us today our daily bread.
All: Forgive us our sins as we forgive those who sin against us. Lead us not into temptation, but deliver us from evil.

Leader: Let us give thanks for God's presence in our lives.

> > *give thanks for times when we have been aware of God;*

> > *rejoice that we go with, not from, God's presence.*

Leader: The kingdom, the power, and the glory are yours,
All: now and for ever. Amen.

>>Get going: prayer practices (5 minutes)

The real value of this course is in moving us to pray *between the sessions*. You may want to share out these activities so that each member tries a different one. Look at the suggestions and share what you would like to try. Come to the next session ready to report any successes, struggles or insights gained.

> **Practise the prayer patterns.** Use *Getting in touch* in a quiet moment during a busy day. When using the Lord's Prayer pattern, focus it on some specific area of need.

> **Read and pray over Psalm 1,** which beautifully, yet starkly, describes the impact of the 'friends we choose' on how we live.

> **Building relationships.** Try to notice what you and others do to deepen relationships. See if this gives you any ideas about how you might deepen your relationship with God in prayer.

> **Try this:**

When you notice during the day that you're feeling good about something, just say it to God, in whatever words come naturally. Similarly, when there's something you feel worried about, like an appointment or an interview. Or when you get news about someone you care about. Don't just feel it – say it. It's like talking to yourself, which we actually do much of the time: you just turn the talk outwards to God.

John Pritchard, How to Pray, *pp. 9-10*

> **A prayer to learn by heart.** We find it much easier to worship God when we know the words of the hymn or song so well that they just flow out of us. That is why it is also good to learn a few key prayers by heart. Here is one:

Collect for purity

Almighty God,
to whom all hearts are open,
all desires known,
and from whom no secrets are hidden:
cleanse the thoughts of our hearts
by the inspiration of your Holy Spirit,
that we may perfectly love you,
and worthily magnify your holy name;
through Christ our Lord. **Amen.**

Common Worship, p. 168

>>Extras

For further reflection, see the supplementary material *Let's be practical,* page 65.

>> 2 Source of Joy: prayer as enjoying God/Beforehand

>>Aim

Prayer involves stepping outside ourselves and our concerns to give attention to God. This includes thanksgiving, celebration and silent adoration. It puts the focus on God rather than on us: paying attention to the *seeing* aspect of the *seeing–knowing–going* pattern in relationships introduced in the previous session.

What you will need (make your own selection)

For the *Do something* section:

> **Option 1:** DVD or video of the film *Truly, Madly, Deeply*;

> **Option 2:** flipchart/lining paper, scissors and PVA glue, magazines and newspapers;

> **Option 3:** a range of objects – pebbles, wood, flowers, pictures of landscapes, a loaf of bread and a glass of wine, objects representing hobbies.

>>Background

Session background: prayer as enjoying God

Worship is the starting point of prayer and everyone in the world is a worshipper. We all, instinctively, 'centre' our lives around something. It may be pleasure, wealth, success, a name for ourselves, having a good time, making poverty history, or supporting a football team. But we all do it. For the Christian the centre is God and to become a Christian, whether suddenly or slowly, is to discover that God rather than self is the true centre. The Reformers used the phrase 'turning in on the self' to define sin. Conversion involves turning round to see God as the centre.

So to worship is to act on that fact. It is to put God in the centre. The goal of worship is not actually to enjoy ourselves, or enjoy the service. The goal is to enjoy God: to give him our full, undivided, attention. We do that in prayer.

Prayer, then, is simply being present to the presence of God.

John Pritchard, How to Pray, *p. 11*

Worship reminds us of the unseen reality of God and the spiritual dimension of life. It is not God who needs our worship, but we who need to worship if we are ever to see things straight. Worship is akin to a blind person rehearsing to him- or herself, while walking down the street, what is all around. It reminds us what is there and what matters. So giving time and attention, indeed love, to God is at the heart of being a Christian. Indeed, it is what it means to be fully human. Jesus, the one who was most fully human, was constantly seeking to give the Father his attention in prayer and worship.

But worship is by no means all one-way. Adoration is about being in the presence of God and enjoying and receiving that reality.

Bible passage background:
Mary anoints Christ (John 12.1-8)

This is the story of two people whose lives had been transformed by Christ. Lazarus, who had been raised from the dead by Christ, honours him and seeks to enjoy his company by throwing a party. He is celebrating the One who brought him back to life.

Mary also comes to celebrate, yet from a very different perspective. She too has been 'raised from the dead' because, in Christ, she has found a source of love that has enriched her, brought her wholeness and restored her to life. She has seen an accepting, life-changing, love and comes to give herself to the source of that love. She does so by giving what she values most – precious ointment. By it she expresses her own self-giving that is unselfconscious in its outpouring at the feet of Christ.

We are told that love is blind, but Mary's love is far-sighted. She glimpses something of what lay ahead for Jesus. She anoints his feet (symbolic of preparation for death, rather than anointing the head, which is for authority): loosens her hair (a sign of deep grief) to wipe his feet. In so doing, Mary blesses Jesus. He sought loving support and understanding from his disciples, who responded by falling asleep then falling away. However, he found the loving attention and support he longed for through Mary's actions.

So the greatest joys (resurrection) and deepest sorrows (death) draw out of Lazarus and Mary an overflowing outpouring of self-giving, generous, love for Christ. So for us, in prayer, we do just that.

Prayer pattern background: resources for worship

Sometimes we might struggle to express our love to God in prayer, for all sorts of reasons. Similarly, we have all had experiences of meeting someone important or wanting to say something loving and affirming to another person, but – when it comes to it – we dry up and miss the moment. It can happen in prayer too. We need to remember that life gives us endless resources to fuel our worship of God: our whole experience of life is a wellspring that need never run dry. It includes . . .

> **The Holy Spirit**, who prays from within us. It is the Spirit who moves us to worship God. 'The Spirit helps us in our weakness' (Romans 8.26, NRSV).

God himself not only longs for us with a passion that far surpasses our wistful yearnings, but the heart of Christian prayer is his praying with us.
Stephen Cottrell, Praying Through Life, *p. 2*

> **The Scriptures**
encounters: e.g. the calls of Abraham (Genesis 12.1-9), Moses (Exodus 3.1-10), Isaiah (Isaiah 6.1-8), Peter (Luke 5.1-11), Bartimaeus (Mark 10.46-52), Zacchaeus (Luke 19.1-10), John (Revelation 1.9-20);
psalms: which are the Church's hymn book: especially, for example, Psalms 8, 19, 30, 33, 34, 40, 46, 66, 67, 93;

> **Music, art, nature, poetry:** watch out for a picture, piece of poetry, film, landscape or sculpture that draws you into worship.

> **Life experiences:** something someone said 'in passing', or something that happened to you, may prompt you to turn to

God. Let it! Relationships can be painful and disappointing, but they are often our greatest source of joy, security, affirmation and stimulus. As such, they can prompt us to give thanks to God.

> **Our emotions/intuitions/aspirations/desires** can be harnessed and drawn on as a source of our praise. Too easily, church worship seems to require leaving both our minds and our emotions at the door. True worship draws on both. They are God-given gifts.

Note: The leader may want to draw on the above worship resources in his or her input to the group, or it may be sufficient simply to point people to this section, at the end of the session, as an aid to personal prayer between sessions.

>> 2 Source of Joy: prayer as enjoying God/The Session

>>Welcome (10 minutes)

Introduction

Welcome people back to the group. This session is about 'seeing' God: that is, giving our full attention to God in thanksgiving, worship and adoration and discovering more of what it means to enjoy God.

Looking back over the time since the last session, share joys and struggles in the use of any of the *prayer practices* suggested then, and any other experiences of prayer. Be honest!

There's something about sunbathing that tells us more about what prayer is like than any amount of religious jargon. When you're lying on the beach or under the lamp, something is happening, something that has nothing to do with how you feel or how hard you're trying. You're not going to get a better tan by screwing up your eyes and concentrating. You give the time, and that's it. All you have to do is turn up. And then things change, at their own pace. You simply have to be there where the light can get at you.

Archbishop Rowan Williams, on Pause for Thought, *BBC Radio 2*
(see Extras *chapter, page 67)*

What do you think, and feel, about that approach to prayer?

>>Drawing near (10 minutes)

Create a still atmosphere. You might like to light a candle, play some music, place an icon or cross as a visual focus and use either, or both, of the *Getting in touch* prayer patterns (see pages 17–18) and/or the course prayer (page 18).

>>Time to share (10 minutes)

Think of someone you know whose company you enjoy.
Why do you enjoy their company?

The Westminster Catechism* says that our chief end is to 'glorify God and enjoy him for ever'. What might be involved for us in enjoying God?

*The Westminster Catechism is a teaching tool of Christian doctrine adopted by the General Assembly of the Church of Scotland in 1648.

>>Encounter (25 minutes)

a. Input: enjoying God (5 minutes)

Using the *Background* material (pages 25–6), introduce the idea of enjoying God.

b. Read (5 minutes)
Mary anoints Jesus (John 12.1-8, NRSV)

See background notes on pages 26–7.

> [1] Six days before the Passover Jesus came to Bethany, the home of Lazarus, whom he had raised from the dead. [2] There they gave a dinner for him. Martha served, and Lazarus was one of those at the table with him. [3] Mary took a pound of costly perfume made of pure nard, anointed Jesus' feet, and wiped them with her hair. The house was filled with the fragrance of the perfume. [4] But Judas Iscariot, one of his disciples (the one who was about to betray him), said, [5] 'Why was this perfume not sold for three hundred denarii and the money given to the poor?' [6] (He said this not because he cared about the poor, but because he was a thief; he kept the common purse and used to steal what was put into it.) [7] Jesus said, 'Leave her alone. She bought it so that she might keep it for the day of my burial. [8] You always have the poor with you, but you do not always have me.'

c. Talk about it (15 minutes)

Consider some or all of the following questions:

> In what ways are Mary and Lazarus centred on Jesus?

> How does Jesus pay attention to them?

> How might we pay attention to Jesus today?

>>Do something (15 minutes)

Try **one** of the following options:

> Watch a clip from the film *Truly, Madly, Deeply*. Introduce the extract with the following information:

Truly, Madly, Deeply *explores the themes of grief, loss and love. Nina (Juliet Stevenson) is grieving over the death of her husband Jamie (Alan Rickman). In the process of moving on, she goes on a first date with Mark (Michael Maloney).*

Watch the film from scene 12 (01.08.00), when Nina apologizes for being late), to scene 12 (01.13.10). Introduce the question before you watch the clip, then discuss in groups:

What can you identify in this meeting that suggests that Nina and Mark might enjoy each other's company and that their relationship could flourish?

> Put group members into groups of two or three. Give each group a piece of paper and access to papers, magazines, pens, etc. Ask them to produce a poster representing the things they enjoy about God.

> Place a variety of objects around the room, such as pebbles, wood, flowers, pictures of landscapes, a loaf of bread and a glass of wine, objects representing hobbies, a range of music CDs. Give people time to move around and explore these items. Now put people into small groups. Ask them to select two items that represent particular enjoyment for them and to share what that enjoyment is and how it speaks to them about enjoying God.

>>Go deep: prayer patterns (10 minutes)
Stepping into worship

Even natural politeness dictates that, when we meet someone, we do not rush in with a list of our needs, but greet the person and pay attention to him or her first. So, in prayer, our first task is to see God rather than ask for anything. This prayer pattern helps us to take natural steps into God's presence. It begins with thanking God for what we have received from him, moves on into worship for what he does and praise for who he is – his nature.

Reaching out beyond ourselves is the first move in prayer.

John Pritchard, How to Pray, *p. 4*

How come most prayers that adults say begin with please, and most prayers children say begin with thanksgiving?

Stephen Cottrell, Praying through Life, *p. 7*

Introducing the prayer pattern

Summarize the introductory paragraph above or let people read it for themselves.

Explain that this prayer pattern is designed to help us to give attention to God.

> Words in ordinary type are said by the leader.

> Words in **bold** are said out loud by all.

> Words in *italics* are prompts for personal prayer, and may be read out by the leader as appropriate.

> Allow silence for personal prayer and reflection between each section.

Stepping into worship

Let us give thanks to God for the good gifts of life . . .

> *our health, faculties, food, clothes, shelter, work;*

> *family, friends, beauty of the world, creativity, leisure.*

Leader: Everything created by God is good.
All: We receive God's gifts with thanksgiving. (1 Timothy 4.4)

Give praise . . . to God for who he is . . .

> *his revelation of himself in Christ, creation, Scripture;*

> *our experience of his mercy, goodness, help, grace.*

Leader: Rejoice in the Lord, always; again I say rejoice.
All: We will rejoice in the Lord at all times. (Philippians 4.4)

Give yourself . . . to God . . .

> *enjoying the wonder of who he is, in silent attentiveness;*

> *offering ourselves to be part of his loving purposes.*

Leader: Present your bodies as a living sacrifice,
All: holy and acceptable to God, which is our spiritual worship.
(Romans 12.1)

>>Get going: prayer practices (5 minutes)

Choose one to try before the next session:

> **Practise the prayer pattern.** Use the *Stepping into worship* exercise at the start of a prayer time. See *Resources for worship*, on pages 27–8 for further help.

> **Read and pray Psalm 100.** It is a celebration of God's goodness in creation and redemption. 'Pray' it by reading it slowly and adding your own 'prayer comments'.

> **Build relationships.** As you meet others, try to see them afresh, noticing things about them. Look for opportunities to pay compliments and affirm the gifts and skills of others.

> **Pay attention to creation.** Notice the world in which you live. Don't take it for granted: receive it with thanksgiving.

Nature constantly amazes us and invites us to respond.
John Pritchard, How to Pray, *p. 12*

> Try this:

Let yourself be stopped in your tracks by things that take your breath away. Don't censor out the moments of wonder and amazement but pause to enjoy the experience and to thank God. It takes practice! Ask God at the start of the day to help you to *see*.

John Pritchard, How to Pray, *p. 56*

> **Take your collection to church.** Prepare for worship by collecting up, in your mind, all that you want to bring to God by way of praise, thanksgiving and delight in him.

> **A prayer to learn by heart.** Hymns and psalms are a rich resource for our prayer to and worship of God.

Hymn of worship

Praise, my soul, the King of heaven!
to his feet your tribute bring;
ransomed, healed, restored, forgiven,
who like me his praise should sing?
Alleluia, alleluia,
praise the everlasting King!

H. F. Lyte (1793–1847)

>>Extras

For further reflection, see supplementary material 2, Archbishop Rowan Williams' *Pause for Thought*, on page 67.

>> 3 Source of Light: prayer as listening/Beforehand

>>Aim

This session explores ways in which we can hear what God is saying to us, through life, art, others and – especially – the Scriptures. It takes us beyond prayer-as-asking God into ways in which God both asks things of us and gives good gifts to us. Within the *seeing–knowing–going* pattern of relationships explored in the first session, this explores something of what is involved in *knowing* God.

What you will need (make your own selection)

For the *Do something* section:

> **For Option 1:** DVD or video of the film *Four Weddings and a Funeral*.

> **For Option 3:** *The Christ we Share* pack, or a range of icon postcards, or download icons via an Internet search engine (images–icons of Christ).

>>Background

Session background: prayer as listening to God

'A friend in need is a friend indeed' – so runs the popular saying. That is certainly the popular understanding of prayer. Prayer is seen as almost exclusively about asking God for help when we are in trouble. However, a friend who is there *only* in times of need is not really a friend. Any relationship involves much more. It is the intimate exchange of knowing and being known. This is true in our relationship with God. God is a God of revelation, not only on the grand scale of creation, the history of Israel, and the great acts of God in Christ, but also in his desire to reveal himself to his people, corporately and individually. As the Scriptures eloquently demonstrate, God is a God-who-speaks.

Prayer is not just about what we ask from God – this is a common misunderstanding – it is about what God asks from us.

Stephen Cottrell, Praying Through Life, *pp. 8, 24*

Bible passage background:
Mary visits Elizabeth (Luke 1.39-45)

There is an urgency about Mary's visit ('went with haste') that is not surprising. She had just been visited by the angel Gabriel and now knows she is pregnant. She had so much to say, and only one person she could think of saying it to. No wonder she stayed three months!

Both women knew their pregnancy was 'of God' yet both would be socially embarrassed: Mary because of her youth and unmarried state, Elizabeth because of her 'advanced years'.

Notice the quality of Elizabeth's listening. She listens to Mary, to her own body and the child in her womb. In it all she listens to God enough to pronounce a beatitude (blessing) specific to Mary.

Prayer pattern background:
listening to the Scriptures

Christ, himself the one described as the Word of God and the Word-made-flesh, saw listening to God as central to what it is to be fully human.

One does not live by bread alone, but by every word that comes from the mouth of God.

Matthew 4.4 (NRSV)

My mother and my brothers are those who hear the word of God and do it.

Luke 8.21 (NRSV)

One of the oldest forms of listening prayer is called *lectio divina*, or divine reading. It was developed in the early monastic communities of the fourth century AD and then became foundational to the Benedictine Order. The four elements to its approach to engaging with the Scriptures are:

> *reading*: slowly with an attentive ear;

> *meditating*: with the whole of our being;

> *praying*: using them to guide our praying;

> *rejoicing*: in the God who speaks.

This pattern is the basis of the prayer pattern *Listening to the Scriptures* on pages 41–3.

Lectio divina is an 'active' kind of reading in this sense:
we are not just passive listeners to what God has said
and done in the past.
The words are addressed to us,
and we are expected to do something.
They are one side of a conversation,
to which our prayer and lives are the response.

David Foster, Reading with God, *p. 1*

>> 3 Source of Light: prayer as listening/The Session

>>Welcome (10 minutes)

This session explores prayer as the way we listen to God. The only way to *know* a person is to spend time with, and listen to, him or her. This too is how we *know* God.

Looking back over the time since the last session, share joys and struggles in the use of any of the *prayer practices* suggested then and any other experiences of prayer. Be honest!

The real work of prayer is to become silent and listen to the voice that says things about me.

Henri Nouwen, Life of the Beloved, *p. 62*

If we really want to pray we must first learn to listen, for in the silence of the heart God speaks.

Mother Teresa of Calcutta, In the Silence of the Heart, *p. 19*

What difficulties do you find in listening to God?
How might we help each other to overcome these difficulties?

>>Drawing near (10 minutes)

Create a still atmosphere. You might like to light a candle, play some music or encourage people to focus on something that speaks of God's peace and presence. See page 10 for suggestions. Alternatively, provide a visual resource such as a cross or image of Christ (see pages 11–12).

Consider using either the *Getting in touch* (pages 17–18) or *Stepping into worship* (pages 32–3) prayer pattern at this point. If using the *Getting in touch* pattern, consider concluding by saying slowly, line by line . . .

Be still and know that I am God
Be still and know that I am . . .
Be still and know . . .
Be still . . .
Be . . .

And/or use the course prayer – see page 18.

>>Time to share (10 minutes)

Explore one (or more, as time allows) of the following:

Think of someone you find it easy to talk with and share things that concern and trouble you. What is it about that person that makes him or her someone you want to talk to?

What, from your experience, do you see as the most important thing about listening to another person? Make a list and share it with the whole group.

Can you recall any recent experiences of sensing God saying something to you? If so, how did it happen and what does it say about how we might best hear God?

>>Encounter (25 minutes)

a. Input: prayer as listening to God (5 minutes)

Use the *Background* material (page 35) to introduce the idea of listening to God in prayer and through reflection on the Scriptures.

b. Read (5 minutes)
Mary visits Elizabeth (Luke 1.39-45, NRSV)

See background notes on page 36.

[39] In those days Mary set out and went with haste to a Judean town in the hill country, [40] where she entered the house of

Zechariah and greeted Elizabeth. [41] When Elizabeth heard Mary's greeting, the child leapt in her womb. And Elizabeth was filled with the Holy Spirit [42] and exclaimed with a loud cry, 'Blessed are you among women, and blessed is the fruit of your womb. [43]And why has this happened to me, that the mother of my Lord comes to me? [44] For as soon as I heard the sound of your greeting, the child in my womb leapt for joy. [45] And blessed is she who believed that there would be a fulfilment of what was spoken to her by the Lord.'

c. Talk about it (15 minutes)

Consider some of or all the following questions:

> We are told that Mary 'went with haste'. *What do you think she is seeking from her meeting with Elizabeth?*

> Look at Elizabeth's response to Mary. *Do you think Mary finds what she is looking for?*

> Mary had just been visited by the angel Gabriel; she listened to the angel's words and her listening prompted action – her visit to Elizabeth. *What other examples from the Scriptures can you think of in which listening to God prompts action?*

> *Can any of us share a story from our own experience in which listening to God prompted action?*

>>Do something (15 minutes)

Try **one** of the following options:

> Watch a clip from the film *Four Weddings and a Funeral*. Introduce the extract with the following information:

Charles (Hugh Grant) is finally on the point of getting married when he begins to doubt that he is marrying the right woman. Unable to express his doubts coherently, he says nothing.

Watch the film from scene 27 (01.39.10), when Charles asks his best man 'What do we think about marriage?'), to scene 27 (01.45.12), when the bride punches him!). Introduce the question before watching the clip, and then discuss in groups:

What can we learn about the nature of genuine listening from the intervention of Charles's deaf brother?

> In groups of three – allocate one person to share with the other two something he or she has found exciting/interesting, for about two to three minutes. One of the listeners is to listen for *information* and the other is to listen to the *feeling* the speaker communicates. The listeners feed back to the speaker, who comments on how well they have listened.

> Scatter images of Christ around the room. Allow people to wander about and examine the images, noting the ones that attract them and any they dislike. Invite people to listen to what God might be saying to them through their responses.

Allow time for people to share their experiences.

>>Go deep: prayer patterns
(10 minutes)
Listening to the Scriptures (lectio divina)

In listening to God through the Scriptures: We are doing more than reading words . . . We are 'listening with the heart to the Holy within'.

Richard Foster, Prayer, *p. 157*

This pattern of prayer involves reading the same passage several times, seeking to develop our ability to listen to what it says, each time.

Well before the meeting, arrange for someone to read the passage (three times). The passage is set out below.

Introducing the prayer pattern
Explain the process in these terms:

> We will be reading the passage three times, with silence for reflection after each reading.

> During **the first reading** we **listen** out for a word or phrase that catches our attention. After some silence we will be invited to speak out that word or phrase. If someone else has said the word or phrase that struck you, it is still important to say it for ourselves too.

During **the second reading** we **reflect** on that word or phrase and on what it is saying to us. After some silence, we will be invited to speak out that reflection – in a word, phrase or no more than a sentence. We do not discuss what anyone shares, just listen and reflect on it.

During **the third reading** we **respond** to that word or phrase by praying to God in the words of, or along the lines of, our reflection.

After some silence, we will be invited to express that response either in silent or spoken prayer. If we are speaking out our prayers, it is best to keep them to a single sentence, perhaps beginning with the words 'We thank you for . . . ' or 'Lord, help us to . . . '.

Finally, without a further reading, we **rejoice** in the God who has shown us something of his nature and his call to us, through this Scripture. Give our praise, thanksgiving and adoration to the One who delights to reveal himself to us – in silence or spoken out.

NB The leader needs to remind the group, at the start of each new section/reading, what we are asked to do in response to *this* reading. The simplest way to do this is to repeat the appropriate paragraph above.

Mary's Song (Luke 1.46-55, NRSV)

46 And Mary said,
'My soul magnifies the Lord,
47 and my spirit rejoices in God my Saviour,
48 for he has looked with favour on the lowliness of his servant.
Surely, from now on all generations will call me blessed;
49 for the Mighty One has done great things for me,
and holy is his name.
50 His mercy is for those who fear him
from generation to generation.
51 He has shown strength with his arm;
he has scattered the proud in the thoughts of their hearts.
52 He has brought down the powerful from their thrones,
and lifted up the lowly;

[53] he has filled the hungry with good things,
and sent the rich away empty.
[54] He has helped his servant Israel,
in remembrance of his mercy,
[55] according to the promise he made to our ancestors,
to Abraham and to his descendants for ever.'

>>Get going: prayer practices
(5 minutes)

Try one of the following before the next session:

> **Practise one or more of the prayer patterns.** There are now
four to choose from. If using *Listening to the Scriptures*,
choose a brief passage of Scripture and practise the steps of
read–reflect–respond–rejoice. Try to do this more than once
before the next session and report back.

> **Read and pray over Psalm 19**, which rejoices that God
speaks to us through creation and Scripture. Thank God for
times when you have sensed God speaking to you in these
ways.

The psalms are a bit like the prayer book of the Bible.
They have always been the prayer book of the Church.
Every human need and every human emotion
can be found in the psalms somewhere . . .

Stephen Cottrell, Praying Through Life, *p. 89*

> **Try this:** Try praying outdoors, and in particular by coming into
close touch with the natural world. Look closely at the flowers,
trees and bushes we easily take for granted. Touch and feel
the physical texture of things and the life pulsing through the
whole of nature. And be deeply thankful. Perhaps take a few
items – leaves, stones, wood – and bring them to your own
special place of prayer as symbols of God's generous creativity.

> **Build relationships:** Listen to others, giving them your whole
attention. Pray for the skill to be a good listener. Share with
someone you trust something that matters to you at present.

> **Something to ponder:**

Within the Christian tradition life is lived as though human beings are continually being addressed or called to in one way or another. The process of nature, the flux of history, all that happens to each individual every twenty-four hours is a 'mighty sum of things forever speaking'.

J. Neville Ward, Five for Sorrow, Ten for Joy, p. 3

> **A prayer to learn by heart:** before reading the Scriptures:

Collect

Blessed Lord,
Who caused all holy Scriptures to be written for our learning:
help us so to hear them,
to read, mark, learn and inwardly digest them
that, through patience, and the comfort of your holy word,
we may embrace and for ever hold fast
the hope of eternal life,
which you have given us in our Saviour Jesus Christ.
Collect for the Last Sunday after Trinity, Common Worship, p. 422

>>Extras

For further reflection, see supplementary material 3, *When prayer seems impossible*, page 68.

>> 4 Source of Wholeness: prayer as honesty/Beforehand

>>Aim

The previous session explored ways of listening to God through the Scriptures. This session considers how we can listen to God in and through the whole of life. A key ingredient here is that of being honest in our praying, both when we know we have done something wrong, as well as when we feel wronged – by God, life or others. This session continues to explore prayer as *knowing* God.

What you will need (make your own selection)

For the *Do something* section:

> **For option one:** DVD or video of the film *The Mission*.

> **For option two:** A copy (or copies) of Rembrandt's painting, *The Return of the Prodigal Son*. This can be obtained:

as a postcard (available in some Christian bookshops);

via the Internet (go to *images – The return of the prodigal son* in an Internet search engine);

on the cover of Henri Nouwen's book, *The Return of the Prodigal Son* (Darton, Longman and Todd, 1992).

> **For option three:** paper and pens.

>>Background . . .

Session background: prayer as honesty

If prayer is a relationship with God rather than a spiritual technique, then real communication is essential. Yet, in human relationships, as well as in relating to God in prayer, we find it difficult to be honest about what we think or feel. This theme of honesty runs through the whole session. We see it wonderfully practised in the Psalms, where the writer is often starkly honest about his feelings, his wishes and about his despair, sometimes even with God.

One form of love destroying dishonesty is our niceness – never speaking our real thoughts and feelings – in areas of disagreement. Where we disagree, we need to push against each other in direct ways rather than in underhanded ways that usually result in mutual bitterness.

Roberta Bondi, To Pray and to Love, p. 107

Bible passage background: a vision of God (Isaiah 6.1-8)

'The year that king Uzziah died' was a traumatic one for the young prophet and the whole nation. Uzziah was one of the good kings of Israel. He reigned for 50 years and was one of the 'greats' of the house of David, along with David and Solomon.

Then Uzziah was struck down with leprosy. It was not only a deadly disease, but one that involved being completely separated from other human beings in a leper colony. It was impossible to be a king and a leper since all lepers were banished from the community. Worst of all, leprosy was seen as the judgement of God. One was an outcast from society and God. All the hope that had been invested in this reign had turned to dust. No wonder Isaiah turned to God at a time like this.

The text does not tell us if he went to the Temple as part of his daily routine, or if he was driven there by despair. Both discipline and despair are valid grounds for turning to God in prayer. What we do know is that God turned up in unmistakable glory.

This *seeing* of the glory of God leads immediately to a fresh *knowing* of who he is before God: 'Woe is me! I am lost . . . my eyes have seen the King, the Lord of hosts!' Note that he sees God as king – the true king – with the power to bring about his purposes. Hope is replacing despair through his seeing God.

Notice that God does not tell Isaiah that he is a man of unclean lips. Isaiah discovers that when he sees his life in the light of God. We discover the same when we meet a really good, loving, honest or generous person – it throws light on our character and choices. Notice that sin is dealt with

– swiftly. 'Now that this has touched your lips, your guilt has departed and your sin is blotted out.' God's goal is not to make us feel guilty but rather to give us strength to play our part in his purposes for the world around us.

When we pray we become ourselves as God always intended us to be. We let go of the illusion our self-image so often creates and enter into a relationship of love where our true self comes to light, knowing it is cherished and valued.

Stephen Cottrell, Praying Through Life, *p. 140*

So the encounter ends not with a feeling of guilt, or even with the gift of forgiveness, but with a call to share in God's loving purposes. True prayer is the source of wholeness for us and others. It results in our *going* in the light of God's call upon our lives.

Prayer pattern background: listening to life ('examen')

The 'examen' (meaning 'examination – of conscience') is an ancient exercise to enable us to reflect on our experience of life, doing so in the presence of the God who loves and understands us fully.

Note the following guidelines:
> It is best not to do a total replay of the period of time under review. Rather, the initial prayer for light is a request that God will illuminate what really matters.
> We need to listen to our moods and feelings.
> The process involves not only identifying what went well or badly, but discerning what our response to this should be. It may be thanksgiving, repentance, tough choices, or forgiveness.

The *examen* is a good prayer to use at the end of the day. Encourage people to use it in that way in the coming days.

>> 4 Source of Wholeness: prayer as honesty/The Session

>>Welcome (10 minutes)

Introduction

This session continues to explore ways in which we *know* God in prayer – not least through our listening to him. In the last session we engaged with ways of listening to God through Scripture. In this session we look at how we can listen to God in the whole of life.

The session introduces an ancient prayer pattern to help us listen to God, called the *examen* (see below for explanation).

Looking back over the time since the last session, share joys and struggles in the use of any of the prayer practices suggested in the last session and any other experiences of prayer. Be honest!

Prayer is no easy matter.
It demands a relationship in which you allow the other
to enter into the very centre of your person,
to speak there, to touch the sensitive core of your being,
and allow the other to see so much
that you would rather leave in darkness.

Henri Nouwen, Seeds of Hope, *p. 66*

What holds us back from being honest with God?

>>Drawing near (10 minutes)

Create a still atmosphere. You might like to light a candle, play some music or encourage people to focus on something that speaks of God's peace and presence. Alternatively, provide a visual resource such as a cross (see pages 11–12). Use either of the prayer patterns *Getting in touch* (pages 17–18), or *Stepping into worship* (pages 32–3) and/or the course prayer (see page 18), here.

Progress in the life of prayer is not about what we achieve, but what we allow ourselves to receive.

Stephen Cottrell, Praying Through Life, *p. 8*

>>Time to share (10 minutes)

Explore one (or more, if time allows) of the following questions, then the final one (in *italics*).

Who are you able to be really honest with? Why?

What are the benefits or difficulties of trying to be honest in our dealings with others?

Whom do you most admire for being able to speak their mind without upsetting everyone? What can you learn from that person?

What can you learn from all this about being honest before God?

>>Encounter (25 minutes)

a. Input (5 minutes)

Using the *Background* material (page 45), introduce the idea of being honest in prayer.

Prayer is relationship with God,
and no relationship, certainly not with the Divine,
exists without emotional honesty.

John Sandford, The Man Who Wrestled with God, *p. 38*

b. Read (5 minutes)
A vision of God (Isaiah 6.1-8, NRSV)

See background notes on pages 46–7.

[1] In the year that King Uzziah died, I saw the Lord sitting on a throne, high and lofty; and the hem of his robe filled the temple. [2] Seraphs were in attendance above him; each had six wings: with two they covered their faces, and with two they covered their feet, and with two they flew. [3] And one called to another and said:

'Holy, holy, holy is the Lord of hosts;
the whole earth is full of his glory.'
[4] The pivots on the thresholds shook at the voices of those who
called, and the house filled with smoke. [5] And I said: 'Woe is me! I
am lost, for I am a man of unclean lips, and I live among a people
of unclean lips; yet my eyes have seen the King, the Lord of hosts!'
[6] Then one of the seraphs flew to me, holding a live coal that had
been taken from the altar with a pair of tongs. [7] The seraph
touched my mouth with it and said: 'Now that this has touched
your lips, your guilt has departed and your sin is blotted out.'
[8] Then I heard the voice of the Lord saying, 'Whom shall I send, and
who will go for us?' And I said, 'Here am I; send me!'

c. Talk about it (15 minutes)

Consider some of or all the following questions:

> The holiness of God causes Isaiah to become acutely aware of
his own failings and those of his people. *What does he do in
response to this awareness and what can we learn from this?*

> *What do we learn about God from this passage?*

> *How does this passage encourage us to pray?*

>>Do something (20 minutes)

Try one of the following options:

> Watch a clip from the film *The Mission*. Introduce the extract
with the following information:

*The following clip focuses on the character of Rodriguez
Mendosa (Robert de Niro) who, having killed his brother and
hidden away for six months, is helped to face the reality of
his sin through an encounter with a Jesuit priest (Jeremy
Irons). Mendosa chooses to carry a huge physical burden as
part of his penance.*

Watch the film from scene 10 (00.34.28), when one of the
priests expresses concern to his superior – Jeremy Irons –

over the severity of Rodriguez's penance, to scene 10 (00.40.45), where Irons embraces the penitent man. Introduce the question before you watch the clip, then discuss in groups:

What does Rodriguez's choice of penance suggest about his honesty with God, with others and with himself? What is the result of his honesty?

> Show an image of Rembrandt's painting – *The Return of the Prodigal Son*. Ask people to look carefully at the painting for five minutes, noting anything that strikes them. Then invite discussion about what this painting has to say about human honesty and God's response.

> In pairs, read Luke 18.10-14. Give the Pharisee and the tax collector a mark out of ten for their degree of honesty with God. Allow time for discussion. Ask pairs to share and explain their marks with the wider group.

>>Go deep: prayer patterns
(10 minutes)

Listening to life (examen)

An examen (Latin for 'examination') is a way of stopping to reflect on and learn from our experience of life, and find God's grace to live life enriched by that reflection. It is classically a prayer for a retreat, but is a good way to end the day. It is also a good way, at the end of each week, to prepare for Sunday worship.

It is suggested that the focus of the use of the examen now is as a personal reflection on the last 24 hours.

It works best if the person leading the group says, either

> the words in *italics*;

> or, these basic ideas, but in their own words;

> or a combination of these two options

as they take the group through this prayer pattern. Allow silence for personal prayer and reflection between each section, informing the group that this is how this pattern will be used here.

Listening to life (examen)

As we look back over the previous 24 hours, let us reflect on our experience of God in life. We take the following steps:

> **1. Thanksgiving:** *let us give thanks to God for his presence with us now and during the period of time under review.*

> **2. Prayer for light:** *let us ask God to guide our reflections and throw light on our recent experience of life.*

> **3. Review:** *This is the heart of the process.*

> > *You do not need to try to remember everything;*

> > *rather, allow the Spirit to prompt and guide your thoughts;*

> > *pay attention to any significant moments and to any feelings of joy, puzzlement, anger, etc.*

> **4. Response:** *respond to God in whatever way seems appropriate. This may be with thanksgiving, confession, delight, commitment to action, or intercession.*

> **5. Looking forward:** *as we look to what lies ahead for us . . . let us consider before God:*

> > *what do I want to give thanks to God for?*

> > *what do I need from God?*

> > *how might God be calling me to live with different attitudes, values and priorities?*

> > *offer yourself to God for the new period of time opening up before you.*

>>Get going: prayer practices
(5 minutes)

Try one of the following before the next session:

> > ***Practise the prayer patterns.*** Remember there are now five to choose from. If you are planning to use the *Listening to life*

(examen), try doing it at the end of the day. Or, do it before you next go to church, as a preparation for worship.

> **Read and pray over Psalm 6.** This psalm wrestles with the internal and external factors that frustrate our wholehearted commitment to God. We can use these words to strengthen our honesty and courage to act.

> **Build relationships:** by using the *examen* as a conversation starter at home, work or with friends: such as . . .
When did I/you feel *most/least* alive this week?
What have I/you been *most/least* happy about today?
What have I/you felt *most/least* grateful for recently?
What has been the *best/worst* thing about this project?
What was today's *high/low* point for me/you?
When did I *most/least* give or receive love today?

Then we need to go on to explore how what we have identified could shape our choices/attitudes in the future.

> **Cultivating honesty.** When disagreeing with others it helps:

not to impute wrong motives to them;

simply to report what we think or feel;

to begin sentences with 'I' not 'you'.

Remember, we cannot be honest to God or others if we do not admit the truth to, and about, ourselves first.

A prayer to learn by heart:

Collect

Almighty God,
in Christ you make all things new:
transform the poverty of our nature by the riches of your grace,
and in the renewal of our lives
make known your heavenly glory;
through Jesus Christ your Son our Lord. Amen.
Collect for the Second Sunday of Epiphany, Common Worship, *p. 384*

>>Extras

For further reflection see supplementary material 4, *Making a good confession,* on page 70.

>> 5 Source of Love: prayer as care/Beforehand

>>Aim

Within the *seeing–knowing–going* framework with which the course began, this session focuses on our *going* with God into his world through *intercession*. In doing so we are connecting with God's loving care for all that he has created.

What you will need (make your own selection)

For the *Do something* section:

> **For Option 1:** DVD or video of the film *Dead Man Walking*;

> **For Option 3:** Flipchart paper and pens.

>>Background

Leaders: please see pages 8–10 for tips on how to use this material.

Session background: prayer as care

This is an aspect of prayer with which we are most familiar – yet often struggle – namely, intercession: asking God for good things to be given or happen to us and others. Here are three words that can help us engage more effectively in intercession.

Hope

Much prayer in Scripture, and Christian experience, comes from seeing the gulf between what is and what could be. The gap between the two is like the physics experiment we may have seen at school when a spark jumps between two leads. Prayer is the God-given energy to move from the grief of what is to the joy of what could be. Hannah praying for a child (1 Samuel 1), Nehemiah (Nehemiah 1), Daniel (Daniel 9) and Jesus (Matthew 23) all grieving for Jerusalem, or Paul's prayer for the Galatians (Galatians 4.19) are all fuelled by a vision of what could be. In our prayer for others we need to let God give us hope and a vision of what could be.

'Your kingdom come': This is serious praying for God's massive attack on all that frustrates his good and loving purposes. Are we ready to join in, and to have him start by working on us?

John Pritchard, How to Pray, *p. 17*

Character

If we could stand back from our prayers for others, just for a moment, we would see how easily we pray for improved circumstances but how difficult we find it to pray for enlarged character. Yet the emphasis in Scripture is much more on character than circumstances. Typical of such an approach are Paul's prayer requests from prison. In over half a dozen he asks for prayer. Once he asks that he may get out, but all the rest are prayers that he may 'boldly declare the gospel' where he is. Our prayers need to be not just about easier circumstances but about a godly response to testing times, that they will result in true holiness. But we had better pray that for ourselves not just for others!

Blessing

Truly to pray for another, whether one individual or a whole continent, is to connect ourselves with the love that flows to all God's creation from a heart of tender compassion. To intercede is to pray God's blessing on others. Aaron's Blessing (Numbers 6.23-26) is a good basis for doing this.

Bible passage background: Jesus and Zacchaeus (Luke 19.1-8)

The Romans were too fearful of the populace and lacked local knowledge to collect taxes themselves so they privatized the process, selling tax franchises to the highest bidder. Tax collectors were required to reach certain quotas; whatever else they demanded was their income. Tax collectors were typically wealthy and unscrupulous. They were feared and despised by all.

Zacchaeus was a 'chief tax collector', which suggests he had a group of tax collectors under his authority. It would mean he had more power, more money and more ostracism from more people.

Clearly there was a spiritual search going on in his life that provoked him to leave his tax collecting and go into a (hostile) crowd looking for Jesus. He wanted to 'see' Jesus, but there is nothing to suggest he had any expectation of Jesus seeing him.

Jesus does not ask if he may come for a meal. He says he must. Nor does Jesus tell him how wrong he has been: Zacchaeus sees that simply by being on the receiving end of Christ's friendship. It was clearly a friendship that transformed him. Christ replaced money as the focus of Zacchaeus's attention. Now likeness to Christ is how Zacchaeus measures success and happiness.

Prayer pattern background: blessing others

Using the Scriptures as a basis for our praying for others is a good discipline and great way to form and 'inform' our praying. For example, praying for others (whether individually or as a group) using the fruit of the Spirit (Galatians 5.22-26), the sevenfold gifts of the Spirit (Isaiah 11.2-3), or the Beatitudes (Matthew 5.3-10) enriches and gives focus to our prayer for them.

Our responsibility is to love (that's what prayer is); God's responsibility is to use that love for the good of others.

John Pritchard, How to Pray, *p. 97*

>> 5 Source of Love: prayer as care/The Session

>>Welcome (10 minutes)

Welcome people back to the group and introduce the theme of intercession – *going* with God into his world with his love – as the subject for this final session.

Looking back over the time since the last session, share joys and struggles in the use of any of the prayer practices suggested then and any other experiences of prayer. Be honest!

There is no real distinction, then, between prayer and action. Prayer is action, because God's energy is released into a situation. Prayer leads to action because we cannot with integrity pray for something which we are not also prepared to do something about.

Stephen Cottrell, Praying Through Life, *pp. 28–9*

What do you make of the last two lines of this quotation?

>>Drawing near (10 minutes)

Create a still atmosphere. You might like to light a candle, play some music or encourage people to focus on something that speaks of God's peace and presence. See page 10 for suggestions. Alternatively, provide a visual resource such as a cross or image of Christ (see pages 11–12).

Use either the *Getting in touch* (pages 17–18) or *Stepping into worship* (pages 32–3) prayer pattern and/or the course prayer (see page 18) at this point.

>>Time to share (10 minutes)

Explore one (or more, if time allows) of the following questions, then the final one (in *italics*):

In Harper Lee's novel, *To Kill a Mockingbird*, Atticus Finch, the lawyer, says this to his young daughter Scout:

> You never really understand a person until you consider things from his point of view – until you climb into his skin and walk around in it.

Think of a time when you have really tried to see things from another's perspective. What helps you to do this?

Think of someone you know who takes a real interest in you. How does that person express this? What can we learn from him or her?

What does that have to say to us about our expressing God's loving care for others?

>>Encounter (25 minutes)

a. Input (5 minutes)

Using the *Background* material (pages 54–5), introduce the idea of expressing loving concern for others through our prayers.

Prayer is letting one's heart become the place where the tears of God and the tears of God's children can merge and become tears of hope.

Henri Nouwen, Seeds of Hope, *p. 68*

---

b. Read (5 minutes)
Jesus and Zacchaeus (Luke 19.1-10, NRSV)

See *Background* notes on pages 55–6 of *Beforehand*.

> [1] He entered Jericho and was passing through it. [2] A man was there named Zacchaeus; he was a chief tax-collector and was rich. [3] He was trying to see who Jesus was, but on account of the crowd he could not, because he was short in stature. [4] So he ran ahead and climbed a sycamore tree to see him, because he was going to pass that way. [5] When Jesus came to the place, he looked up and said to him, 'Zacchaeus, hurry and come down; for I must stay at your house today.' [6] So he hurried down and was happy to

welcome him. [7] All who saw it began to grumble and said, 'He has gone to be the guest of one who is a sinner.' [8] Zacchaeus stood there and said to the Lord, 'Look, half of my possessions, Lord, I will give to the poor; and if I have defrauded anyone of anything, I will pay back four times as much.' [9] Then Jesus said to him, 'Today salvation has come to this house, because he too is a son of Abraham. [10] For the Son of Man came to seek out and to save the lost.'

c. Talk about it (15 minutes)

Consider some of or all the following questions:

> Imagine you know someone like Zacchaeus (perhaps you do!). How might you feel about that person? How would you pray for them?

> Jesus surprises the people's expectations by inviting himself to dinner at Zacchaeus's house. In what ways does God's loving concern for the world surprise our expectations?

> Jesus said, 'For the Son of Man came to seek out and to save the lost.' Who are the lost? How does God reach out to the lost today?

>>Do something (20 minutes)

Try **one** of the following options:

> Watch a clip from *Dead Man Walking*. Introduce the extract with the following information:

Sister Helen Prejean became the spiritual advisor to death row convicts at Louisiana's Angola State Penitentiary in 1981. Her experiences formed the basis for her novel and for the film Dead Man Walking. *The film depicts Helen's work with Matthew Poncelet, a complex man convicted of brutal murder and rape and awaiting execution.*

Watch the film from scene 7 (00.49.00), when Hope's mother says, 'Let's go in the kitchen, I'll make ya some coffee' to scene 7 (00.52.20), where Helen drives away from their house). Introduce the question before watching the clip, then discuss in groups:

Do you think Helen Prejean is open to similar criticisms as those aimed at Jesus in the story of Zacchaeus?
What do you think of her work?

> In small groups, list as many examples as you can, from the Scriptures, of God subverting human expectation in his dealings with the world. For example, in the book of Jonah, God calls a Gentile people, the Ninevites, to repentance; and, in healing on the Sabbath, Jesus turns upside down the expectations of the religious authorities. How many similar examples can you find?

> In groups, using a large sheet of paper, draw up a list of five issues (global and/or local) about which people feel a sense of concern. Take each issue in turn and discuss practical and realistic responses to these issues that demonstrate God's loving care.

>>Go deep: prayer patterns
(10 minutes)
Praying God's blessing on others

This prayer pattern uses Aaron's Blessing (Numbers 6.24-26). Before using it, decide together:

> what the focus for your prayer will be. You might want to pray for local church leaders, or national leaders, for those caught up in drug or alcohol abuse, or those working with some of the most deprived people of the world to 'make poverty history';

> whether the personal prayer response is to be silent or spoken out. Do what best fits the group.

Words in ordinary type are said by the leader.

[Words in square brackets are not to be read out but are for the guidance of the leader.]

Words in **bold** type are said by all.

Words in *italics* may be used by the leader as prompts if appropriate.

Aaron's Blessing (Numbers 6.24-26, NRSV)

[Read this out loud, before beginning the prayer pattern.]

> The Lord bless you and keep you;
> the Lord make his face to shine upon you,
> and be gracious to you;
> the Lord life up his countenance upon you,
> and give you peace.

Leader: see this person/situation and bring them/it before God in our imagination:

> see God as active in the circumstances of this person;
> express your longing in terms of 'May God give you . . .'

Leader: May our heavenly Father
All: bless you and keep you.

Leader: Imagine Christ turning to this person as he did to Zacchaeus:

> rejoice in Christ's loving attitude to this person/group;
> pray for the coming of his kingdom in this situation in terms of 'May Christ guide you to . . .'

Leader: May our Lord Jesus Christ
**All: make his face to shine upon you,
and be gracious to you.**

Leader: Rejoice that the Holy Spirit makes Christ known:

> pray that the Spirit's action may be evident and recognized;
> pray for an experience of God's grace in terms of 'May the Holy Spirit strengthen you to . . .'

Leader: May the Holy Spirit
**All: Lift up the light of his countenance upon you,
and give you peace.**

Conclude by praying together the Lord's Prayer:

> Our Father in heaven,
> hallowed be your name,
> your kingdom come,
> your will be done,
> on earth as in heaven.
> Give us today our daily bread.
> Forgive us our sins
> as we forgive those who sin against us.
> Lead us not into temptation
> but deliver us from evil.
> For the kingdom, the power,
> and the glory are yours
> now and for ever. Amen.

Common Worship, p. 36

So this is the purpose of prayer. It is about making the whole of life an offering of praise to God. We do this by developing regular and appropriate patterns of prayer and the fruits of this will be lives that radiate the love of God.

Stephen Cottrell, Praying Through Life, *p. 143*

>>Get going: prayer practices
(5 minutes)

End the session by sharing together:

> How you have benefited from this course.

> How you feel you have moved forward in your prayer life.

> What you will take with you from this course.

Although the course ends at the conclusion of this session, it will not have been effective if we cease to pray now the course is over. What follows are steps we can take beyond the end of the course to continue the learning process, which, we hope, has already breathed new life into our prayer to God. Here are some things we can practise in the future to develop our intercession for others. Whatever you choose, keep doing it!

> **Practise the prayer patterns:** especially *praying God's blessing* on those you love and on the needy areas of the world – people and places that cry out for mercy and hope.

> **Read and pray over Psalm 67:** a psalm overflowing with a hope-filled vision for the whole nation and people of God.

> **Build relationships:** by seeking to enter into other people's world, see life from their perspective and understand why their hopes and griefs are what they are. Then pray for them.

> **Try this:**

Think about the rhythms and routines of your daily life and make time for God by discerning where in each day is your time and place of prayer.
Stephen Cottrell, Praying Through Life, *p. 39*

> **Be open to God:** and what he might be calling us to do to become part of the answer to our prayers.

> **Try this:**

Try a 'handful of prayer'. The five (or ten) fingers and thumbs can each represent a special person you want to pray for. Anywhere, anytime, you can then call to mind those five people and pray for them, placing them 'in the palm of God's hand' (Isaiah 49.16).
John Pritchard, How to Pray, *p. 34*

Prayer is essentially practical. It should make us more human, not less. It should give us resources to live our lives more fully...
John Pritchard, How to Pray, *p. 14*

> **A prayer to learn:**

Living the two great commandments
Eternal God and Father,
you create and redeem us by the power of your love:
guide and strengthen us by your Spirit,
that we may give ourselves in love and service
to one another and to you;
through Jesus Christ our Lord. **Amen.**

Common Worship: Daily Prayer, *p. 142*

>>Extras

For further reflection, see supplementary material 5, *Ten golden rules* on page 72.

>> Extras

This supplementary material may be photocopied for group members or downloaded from the web site: www.chpublishing.co.uk/lifesource.

>>1. Let's be practical

No relationship works if we do not devote time to enjoying and working at it: so too in our prayer relationship with God. So . . .

> Establish *a regular time for prayer*. Temperaments, and work and family schedules are so varied that there is no universal 'right time'. For some it will be at the start of the day, for others at the end. Others may find two or three times a week works best. Keep it brief and achievable (15 to 30 minutes at first) rather than daunting and unattainable. Then let it expand as your prayer life develops.

> *Find a place to pray*. Where you will not be interrupted and where you can have a Bible, a cross, icon, hymn book, etc., to help you.

> *Find a pattern that works for you*. ACTS is one such pattern – Adoration, Confession, Thanksgiving, Supplication. The *seeing–knowing–going* framework used in this course is another. Or you might want to use a liturgical framework such as *Common Worship: Daily Prayer* or *Time to pray*, or one of the many other 'orders'.

> *Keep a balance between form and freedom*. Liturgies, hymns, set prayers are a great aid (especially in difficult times), but we need to use our own words and express our real feelings to God. A diet of all set prayers, or all spontaneous prayers, is likely to prove unbalanced: find room for both on your prayer menu.

> *Ring the changes*. However comfortable you are with your pattern of prayer, take a break from time to time. Holidays are a great time to try something different. You will come back spiritually refreshed!

> *Pray through the day*. God is always present, so . . .

Use natural 'pause' times, such as waiting for the kettle to boil, or driving to work, as prompts for prayer.

Turn your emotions into prayers. Don't just feel it, pray it!

Turn the inner dialogue up to God. We all talk to ourselves through the day. Let God in on this conversation.

Bless others: whose lives you touch – the harassed mother in the shop or the difficult boss. Pray a blessing on them.

>>2. Archbishop Rowan Williams' Pause for Thought

Well, Terry, I don't know how well placed I am, but [what] I do know is that many people find difficulty with prayer. It's one thing to talk about it but quite another to do it; and one of the questions I've often been asked is 'Have you any tips on how to pray?' Let me put it this way: I'm not much of a one for sunbathing; too much lying around and I get fidgety and a bit guilty. But there's something about sunbathing that tells us more about what prayer is like than any amount of religious jargon.

When you're lying on the beach or under the lamp, something is happening, something that has nothing to do with how you feel or how hard you're trying. You're not going to get a better tan by screwing up your eyes and concentrating. You give the time, and that's it. All you have to do is turn up. And then things change, at their own pace. You simply have to be there where the light can get at you.

People often have the impression that praying is anxiously putting on your best clothes, finding acceptable things to say in the right sort of language, generally getting your act together – oh! and concentrating, of course. But when in the Bible Jesus advises his friends about how to pray, he tells them not to worry about any of this. Say, 'Father', he tells them. Just be confident that you're welcome as you would be at home. All you need to do is to be where the light can get at you – in this case, the light of God's love.

Give the time and let go of trying hard (actually this is the difficult bit). God is there always. You don't need to fight for his attention or make yourself acceptable. He's glad to see you. And he'll make a difference while you're not watching, just by radiating who and what he is in your direction. All he asks is that you stay there with him for a while, in the light. For the rest, you just trust him to get on with it.

Broadcast Tuesday 18 October 2005 on the Terry Wogan Show,
BBC Radio 2

>>3. When prayer seems impossible

There are two possible reasons why we might face a time of
darkness in our faith, when we hold out our hand and it does not
feel as if it is being held. The first arises from events in our lives.
Something happens in our life – the death of a loved one, a
serious illness, the loss of our job, the approach of our own death
– that brings us face to face with issues about ourselves and about
life that we had kept hidden. Sometimes this manifests itself in
what feels like a loss of faith. We feel angry and resentful towards
God. It feels as if God has let us down, or even abandoned us.
Prayer feels impossible or suddenly feels useless. God is absent.

The second is often a work of God himself. For no particular reason
prayer becomes empty, familiar words and rituals lose their
comfort, church becomes boring, other Christians irritating, and
faith suddenly feels a ridiculous charade. Something seems to be
sapping the energy of our faith and we feel dried up.

The first thing to say is that both experiences are normal and, for
most people, inevitable. Spiritual writers often speak of these
experiences as being like a desert.

In Christianity the desert is a place of discovery. The people of
Israel are led through the desert into the promised land. Jesus
begins his ministry being driven into the wilderness. The garden of
resurrection is entered through Calvary. Even though the reasons
for experiencing this desert of the faith are different, often the
consequences are similar. If something has happened in our life to
make God feel absent, God can use that experience to nurture in
us a deeper understanding of his constant presence. If we are
going through a period of spiritual dryness, even if we do not know
the reason, we need to begin to trust that God is leading us
through this experience to a deeper understanding of his
overflowing love. What troubles me is that so many Christians are
ill-prepared for the dark times that will inevitably come. I feel that
many people not only give up on prayer, but give up on God when

they find themselves in the desert, because they were never told
that this is a necessary part of faith.

Stephen Cottrell, Praying Through Life, *pp. 127–8*

>>4. Making a good confession

Many of us have to confess to not being good at confession! We are not sure what to confess or how to do it. We end up feeling more guilty than forgiven. How can we 'make a good confession'?

True guilt

There are plenty of sources of *false* guilt . . .

> **from around us**: avoid making others feel guilty; and spot it when anyone is trying to control you by making you feel guilty.

> **from below**: Satan accuses the saints 'day and night before our God' (Revelation 12.10). It usually results in a vague sense of guilt, without any clear focus. It is like being in a fog. Learn to spot it.

> **from within**: too easily we spend time putting ourselves down and 'giving ourselves a hard time'. It's a form of *false* humility.

Holiness is all that reflects the character of God. Sin is all that contradicts his nature, not least our managing by ourselves.

How to repent

Let God do the accusing. This is the wonderful insight of the psalmist that can be a great source of wholeness for us:

Search me, O God, and know my heart;
test me and know my thoughts.
See if there is any wicked way in me,
and lead me in the way everlasting.

Psalm 139.23-24 (NRSV)

Be open to God; don't dig around – let him do the searching. We are simply to open our hearts to this divine health check.

Making a good confession

Take the following steps:

> *admit to God* what has been wrong;

> *be specific* – and do not make excuses;

> *hand it over to God* and let go of it: don't keep going over it;
> *receive forgiveness: God's gift.* Hold on to that, not the past;
> *go on your way rejoicing* – that you are forgiven.

Remember God's goal: it is not to make us feel guilty but to know we are forgiven, and so able to join in with his loving purposes.

>>5. Ten golden rules

1. Start. The hardest thing about prayer is beginning. So just start. Your longing for God, and your wanting to pray, are the beginning of a relationship that can grow and grow. Tell God that you want to know him and love him, and let him make the next move.
2. Invite the Holy Spirit to pray in you and to teach you to pray.
3. Find time to pray. Set aside special times for prayer.
4. Find people to pray with, especially your family, but also friends and work mates. We need one another's support. Remember, there is no such thing as private prayer, we are surrounded by the prayers of others.
5. Build prayer into the rhythms of life.
6. Make your home a place of prayer.
7. Find the way of praying that is right for you. Explore different ways of praying. Listen as well as speak; give thanks as well as make requests. Try to make sure your prayer is marked by adoration, contrition, thanksgiving and supplication, but don't let particular methods get in the way.
8. Don't look for results.
9. Make your life a prayer. Use your times of prayer to make the whole of life prayerful.
10. Don't give up when it gets hard. Trying to pray is praying, and God is present even in the darkness.

Stephen Cottrell, Praying Through Life, *pp. 132–3*

>> Bibliography
and further Resources

Archbishops' Council, *Common Worship: Services and Prayers for the Church of England*, Church House Publishing, 2000.

Archbishops' Council, *Common Worship: Daily Prayer*, Church House Publishing, 2005.

Roberta Bondi, *To Pray and to Love*, Burns and Oates, 1991.

Stephen Cottrell, *Praying Through Life* (second edn), Church House Publishing, 2003.

S. Cottrell, S. Croft, J. Finney, F. Lawson and R. Warren, *Emmaus: Leading an Emmaus Group*, Church House Publishing, 1998, second edition 2004.

David Foster, *Reading with God*, Continuum, 2005.

Richard Foster, *Prayer*, Hodder & Stoughton, 1992.

Harper Lee, *To Kill a Mockingbird*, Heinemann, 1960.

Henri Nouwen, *Seeds of Hope*, Darton, Longman & Todd, 1989.

Henri Nouwen, *Life of the Beloved*, Hodder & Stoughton, 1992.

Elizabeth Obbard, *To Live is to Pray*, Canterbury Press, 1997.

John Pritchard, *How to Pray*, SPCK, 2002.

John Sandford, *The Man who Wrestled with God*, Paulist Press, 1981.

Mother Teresa of Calcutta, *In the Silence of the Heart*, SPCK, 1983.

Time to Pray, Church House Publishing, 2006.

J. Neville Ward, *Five for Sorrow, Ten for Joy*, Darton, Longman & Todd, 1993.

Robert Warren, *An Affair of the Heart* (second edn), Highland, 1999.

Filmography

Roland Joffe (director), *The Mission*, Warner Brothers, 1986.

Anthony Minghella (director), *Truly, Madly, Deeply*, BBC/Samuel Goldwyn Co., 1991.

Mike Newell (director), *Four Weddings and a Funeral*, Channel 4/Gramercy Pictures/Polygram/Working Title Films, 1991.

Tim Robbins (director), *Dead Man Walking*, Gramercy Pictures, 1995.

E is for discipleship

Running Alpha, Christianity Explored or another Christian basics course and struggling to know what to do next? Looking for small group material that's not mind-bogglingly academic or mind-numbingly shallow? Help is at hand.

The 'Emmaus – the Way of Faith' discipleship material offers a library of stand-alone modules that are designed to help Christians develop and grow. Each module is split into four or five sessions which provide material for Bible study, discussion, group exercises, meditations, practical application and prayers. There's plenty of background material for leaders and a series of downloadable handouts for each member of the study group.

Emmaus encourages a journey of faith that is life-changing, enduring and that has a positive impact on the community of believers, as well as the individual.

 Curious? Call 020 7898 1451 today and request a FREE Introduction to Emmaus Pack, email emmaus@c-of-e.org.uk or visit **www.e-mmaus.org.uk** for full details.

Emmaus – the first word in discipleship